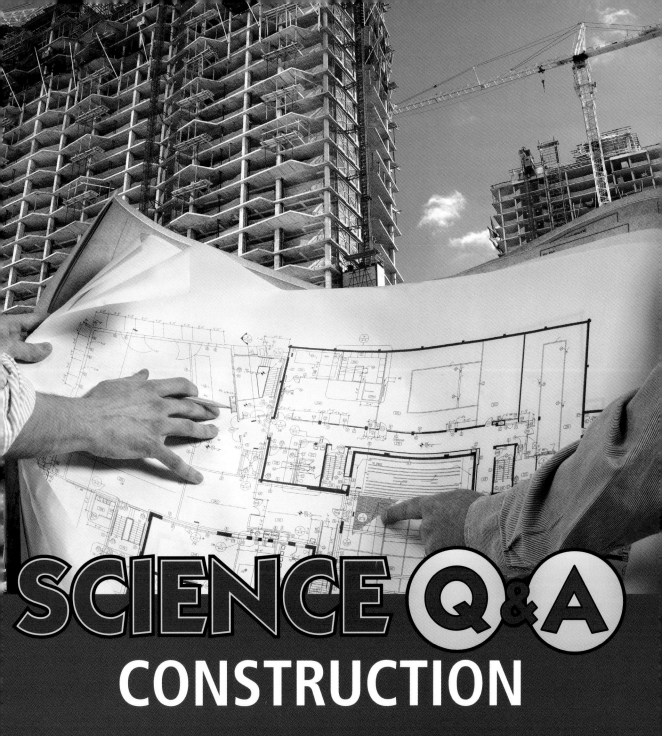

SCIENCE Q&A

CONSTRUCTION

— Rennay Craats —

Weigl Publishers Inc.

Published by Weigl Publishers Inc.
350 5th Avenue, Suite 3304, PMB 6G
New York, NY 10118-0069

NOV 0 5 2008

Website: www.weigl.com

Library of Congress Cataloging-in-Publication Data

Craats, Rennay.
  Construction / Rennay Craats.
      p. cm. -- (Science Q & A)
  Includes index.
  ISBN 978-1-59036-956-2 (hard cover : alk. paper) -- ISBN 978-1-59036-957-9 (soft cover : alk. paper)
  1. Building--Juvenile literature. 2. Structural engineering--Juvenile literature. I. Title.
  TH149.C728 2009
  690--dc22
                          2008003819

Printed in China
1 2 3 4 5 6 7 8 9 0 12 11 10 09 08

Project Coordinator
Heather Hudak

Design
Terry Paulhus

Photo credits

Weigl acknowledges Getty Images as its primary image supplier.

Every reasonable effort has been made to trace ownership and to obtain permission to reprint copyright material. The publishers would be pleased to have any errors or omissions brought to their attention so that they may be corrected in subsequent printings.

CONTENTS

What is a structure?

A structure is almost anything that is built, from a birdhouse to an office building. In some countries, land is precious and scarce. Rather than having wide, one-story homes such as those found on ranches in Texas, some areas are more likely to have tall, thin buildings, which can accommodate many people in a small area.

In the 1800s and early 1900s, many structures were built by hand, with only small tools. Today, construction crews use million-dollar machines and computer-generated designs to help them build structures. They use **synthetic** materials that are more affordable and durable than natural materials. At one time, it was difficult to erect a two-story building. Now, the incredible task of assembling 100 floors on top of each other to build a skyscraper is common practice in construction.

Certain building principles, such as rules that ensure structures are stable and durable, have changed little over time.

What are some of the first structures?

People have been designing unique structures for thousands of years. The best examples of early designs are the pyramids of Egypt. Some of these incredible structures have been standing for about 4,500 years.

find it quick

Learn more about the history and construction of the pyramids. Visit **www.historyforkids.org/learn/egypt**, and click on "Egyptian Architecture (Pyramids)."

The pyramids served as tombs for ancient Egyptian pharaohs. Building them must have been very difficult at the time. The mysteries surrounding the pyramids and their construction make it a remarkable accomplishment.

Historians estimate that between 20,000 and 30,000 people worked nonstop for about 30 years to finish the Great Pyramid at Giza, near Cairo, Egypt. Each side of the base spans 755 feet (230 meters), and the Great Pyramid towers 479 feet (146 m) high.

To complete the structure, more than two million blocks of stone were assembled.

■ The Great Pyramid of Khufu was 25 feet (7.6 m) taller when it was originally built. The outer limestone layer was removed to construct other buildings in Cairo.

The stones of the outer pyramid weigh about 5,000 pounds (2,250 kilograms) each. The ancient Egyptians used huge rollers to carry the blocks to the site, levers to lift them, and ramps to move the blocks to the top of the pyramid.

Today, builders have much different ways to plan and construct buildings.

The long haul

The materials used to build the pyramids of Giza came from near and far. Limestone for the base and the outside part of the pyramid came from just across the Nile River. Copper was brought from eastern Egypt, granite was hauled from southern Egypt, and cedar was shipped across the Mediterranean Sea from Lebanon.

How do builders plan a structure?

Contractors, builders, and engineers on a construction site rely on plans called blueprints. A blueprint is a diagram that shows where interior walls, doors, windows, electrical wiring, and plumbing will be.

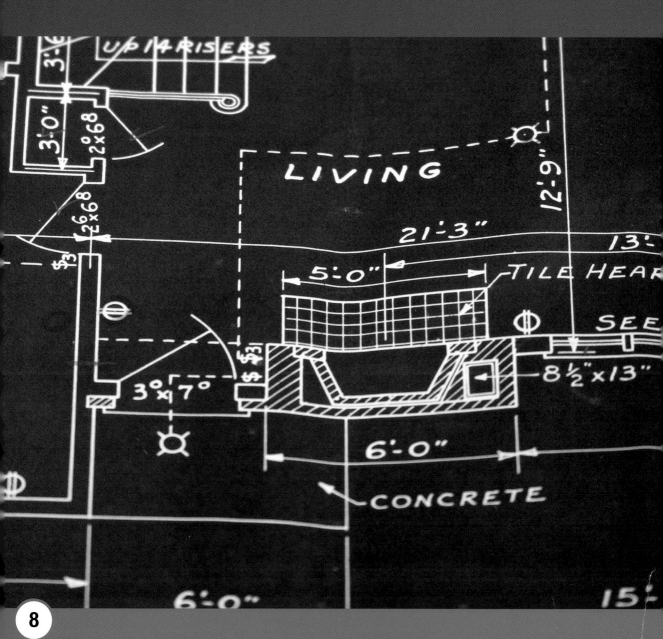

Blueprints are usually large sheets of paper with blue lines outlining the design. They are made by transferring drawings onto paper that has been treated with light-sensitive chemicals.

Blueprints provide exact information to the builder. A few of the components included on a blueprint are the engineering and safety requirements, measurements, and a list of the particular materials that are required for the project.

A building could not be built without blueprints. Construction workers follow the detailed plan on the blueprint to build exactly what the architect imagined for a structure.

A scale is a part of every blueprint. This measurement lets builders know precisely how large the finished building will be.

For many years, architects would draw blueprints by hand. Today, most blueprints are created using computers.

■ Whiteprints, images of blue, brown, or black lines on a white background, are easier to change and read than traditional blueprints.

Here is your challenge!

Make a blueprint of your bedroom. Use a tape measure the length of the walls in your room. Record your measurements. Be sure to mark where the wall is broken by a door or closet.

Next, decide on a scale for your blueprint. For example, 1 inch (2.5 centimeters) on your blueprint could represent 1 foot (0.3 m) in your bedroom. Using a ruler, draw the walls and door according to your measurements.

Finally, map out where the heating vents and electrical outlets are located. This will give you a basic floor blueprint of your bedroom. You can also measure your furniture. Use your scale to convert the measurements, and include your furniture in your floor plan.

Can you see a structure before it is built?

Recently, professionals in the construction industry have started using computers as a tool in their work. Previously, blueprints and small-scale models were the only tools used to help clients visualize what the finished structure would look like.

find it quick

To take a virtual tour of one of the world's most luxurious hotels, the Burj Al Arab, visit **www.burj-al-arab.com**.

Construction companies and architects can use computer software to take clients on a virtual tour of proposed buildings. The digital images created by the computer appear three-dimensional, and sometimes even include furniture. People can see a room from every angle.

If the structure has already been built, virtual tours can be even more detailed. In this case, special cameras photograph each wall in a room. The images are fed into a computer and grouped together to create one large, seemingly three-dimensional photograph of the space.

Another benefit of virtual tours is their convenience. Construction companies or architectural firms can post their "tours" on the Internet. When clients are ready to visit a project in progress, they do not need to travel very far. They just visit the companies' websites.

■ Virtual tours allow people to view buildings they may otherwise never have a chance to see.

How do builders choose a structure's style?

Styles are recycled over time. Buildings in a particular location that were built during the same time period tend to share certain architectural qualities.

Many factors contribute to style, from local materials, to the function the structure will serve, to the owners' individual tastes. During the 17th and 18th centuries, American architects often borrowed styles from European architects. Among those borrowed styles were brick homes that had two identical halves. Other European styles were reflected in the **plantation** homes of the American South. These were enormous structures with simple fronts, open spaces, and large columns on either side of the doorway.

Other countries influenced architecture in the United States until the late 1800s. At this time, American architects began adding their own touches and **innovations**. These included shingles on country houses and metal frames for tall structures that would tower high in the air. Through the years, many styles have come back in fashion.

While these buildings sometimes look the same as older structures, modern machines have been used to build them.

■ Homebuilders often design homes that include elements of Roman or Greek architecture, such as columns. Designers continue to merge styles from centuries ago with the newest design ideas and innovations to create American architecture.

Here is your challenge!

Use your imagination to design a unique structure. You may want to use innovative designs to give your building a different look. Are there any old building styles that might look nice with your design? You can mix the old with the new to design a creative, functional structure.

When should old buildings be protected?

Are you interested in how people lived in the past? Have you ever visited a historic home or building? Do you think modern buildings are better than older buildings?

Around the world, people celebrate their history and try to preserve its physical remains. In the United States, people establish museums in pioneer homes to show how their ancestors lived and worked. In other cases, tours are taken through homes built in the 1800s and early 1900s to experience the past.

The historical buildings in many places are protected by organizations and governments. These groups want to see that the remaining buildings stay intact. Often, groups will restore historical buildings so they look just as they did when they were first built. Sometimes, people do not consider the historical value of a building until there is a threat to tear it down. Then, groups rally together to save a piece of an area's heritage.

Some people believe historical buildings should be torn down. They push for progress. To many, progress means replacing the old with the new. They feel that old buildings may need to be demolished, often because they are run-down and barely standing. By removing these buildings, some developers argue, new life and prosperity can be brought to an area.

■ Historical buildings in remote areas, such as abandoned mines, often fall apart over time. These buildings are reclaimed by nature.

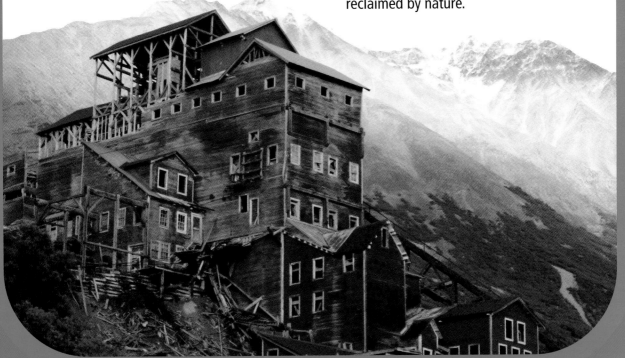

How are old buildings cleared to build new ones?

Construction crews often have to demolish old buildings to make room for new ones. Small buildings, such as houses, can be leveled with wrecking balls and bulldozers. Demolition crews are brought in when large buildings, such as skyscrapers, must be removed from a building site.

find it quick

You can learn more about building demolition by checking out www.implosionworld.com.

■ A building that took months, or even years, to build can be explosively demolished in seconds.

Demolition crews use explosives to safely bring down large buildings. Demolition experts, often called blasters, use blueprints to map the placement of powerful explosives in a large building. They visit the building many times to study how it was built and how they can collapse it. Many blasters create three-dimensional computer models of the building to simulate their plans.

Once the blasters are sure of their plan, they prepare to demolish the building. The key to a successful demolition is to control how the building falls once the explosives have been **detonated**. Many times, old buildings are surrounded by new ones, so demolition crews need to make sure they collapse the building into itself. **Imploding** buildings is challenging work, and there are only a few companies in the world that can do it.

Explosive record

The largest building ever explosively demolished was the Sears Merchandise Center in Philadelphia, Pennsylvania. The building, opened in 1919, measured 2.7 million square feet (250,838 sq m). It was destroyed by 12,000 pounds (5,443 kg) of explosives.

What machines are used to build structures?

Bulldozers, forklifts, cranes, and backhoes are common machines on a construction site. These machines all operate on the principles of hydraulics.

■ There are about one million forklifts in use in the United States. Hydraulics help these machines push, pull, lift, load, unload, and stack materials.

A hydraulic system has two **pistons** in cylinders filled with an **incompressible** liquid, often oil. The oil is pumped to the cylinders and pistons through valves. The pistons are connected by a pipe. When pressure is applied to one piston, the force is transferred to the second piston through the oil. As one piston is pushed down, the other is lifted by the oil. This back-and-forth movement powers the machine. Hydraulic systems in any machine work the same way.

Hydraulics systems are highly flexible because the pipe connecting the pistons can be of any length. It can even be bent to fit around corners. The incompressible oil will still move the pistons. Changing the size of one piston and cylinder creates even more force and power.

Putting on the brakes

Hydraulics can be used for much more than construction. Everyday devices, such as car brakes, use hydraulics. More scientific uses for hydraulics include launching systems for NASA space shuttles and deep sea exploration. The wreckage of the *Titanic* was found using a hydraulic-powered submarine.

How is land prepared for building?

There is one main challenge to building a structure—how to prepare land for building. Bulldozers and hydraulic shovels are two machines commonly used for clearing land.

Before building on a site, the land must be cleared of debris. Bulldozers clear dirt and rocks away from an area, smoothing it out for building. Bulldozers are also used to remove large obstacles, such as trees, from the area. The site is made flat and level before hydraulic shovels are used.

Hydraulic shovels use two pistons—one at the elbow of the shovel's arm and another to turn the bucket. These pistons work with motors to operate the digging and rotating motion of the shovel.

Hydraulic shovels are enormous and complex. Some shovels can weigh nearly 30 tons (27 tonnes) and can remove more than 35 cubic feet (1 cubic m) of dirt at a time. This dirt can weigh up to 1.5 tons (1.36 t). Despite this weight, the shovel can move quickly and easily. The holes dug by hydraulic shovels are filled with concrete to form the structure's foundation, or base.

■ A hole that would take weeks to dig by hand can be dug in a matter of hours by a hydraulic shovel.

Dig a big hole

A standard hydraulic shovel stands about 11 feet (3.3 m) high and is about 35 feet (10.7 m) long.

What is treated lumber?

Wood is a common building material for houses. It is easy to cut and use. Many problems can arise when building with wood because it is a natural material. To avoid these problems, lumber companies produce pressure-treated wood.

To pressure-treat wood, planks of wood are soaked in a liquid preservative, which contains a substance that prevents organisms from settling in wood. This preserves, or makes the wood last longer. After the wood is covered in the preservative, it is put into a pressure chamber. The action of the pressure chamber pushes the preservative into the wood. This ensures that all of the wood is treated.

Pressure-treated wood can last for decades, even when exposed to sunlight, water, and wind. However, people must be careful with pressure-treated wood. It should never be burned in a bonfire, because the wood will release toxic chemicals. It is important to use gloves and avoid breathing in the sawdust when working with or cutting pressure-treated wood.

■ The chemical treatment in pressure-treated wood keeps insects, rodents, and fungus from making homes in the wood.

Feeling the pressure

Pressure-treated wood conserves natural resources by extending the lifespan of the wood. Fewer trees must be chopped down because wooden materials do not need to be replaced as often.

How are cement and concrete used?

Although the words "cement" and "concrete" are often used to describe the same substance, they are not the same thing. Cement is a gray powder. It is one of the ingredients used to make concrete. Concrete is a hard building material that is made by mixing cement, sand, small stones, and water.

Concrete was invented thousands of years ago by the Romans. They used concrete to build arches, domes, and roads. The Egyptians used concrete to make columns more than 3,600 years ago.

In 1824, a British inventor named Joseph Aspdin invented a special kind of cement called Portland cement. Today, it is the key ingredient used in most types of concrete because it works like a glue, holding the concrete together. It makes concrete that is much stronger and more versatile than earlier forms of concrete. Today, concrete made from Portland cement is used to make dams, bridges, buildings, and pavement.

To make Portland cement, materials such as clay, limestone, and sand are crushed

■ On average, a cement truck can carry up to 40,000 pounds (18,144 kg) of cement.

together and poured into a large oven called a kiln. The materials inside the kiln reach temperatures between 2,700° and 3,000° Fahrenheit (1,480° and 1,650° Celsius). This incredible heat causes the ingredients to break down and form into new substances.

After it is removed from the kiln, the cement is mixed with water to produce concrete. Then it is brought to the construction site in a special truck that has a rotating barrel. The barrel moves constantly to keep the concrete from hardening. Once poured, the surface of the concrete is kept damp so that it can cure, or harden. The longer the concrete is allowed to cure, the stronger it will be.

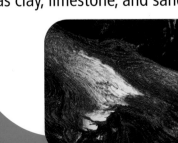

Hot water

Ancient Romans used a type of volcanic ash, called *pozzolana*, from Mount Vesuvius, to make cement that would harden under water.

What are simple machines?

Not all machines on a construction site tower over the people operating them. Simple machines are important in construction. These machines make tasks easier because they use only one movement to do a job.

find it quick

Learn about simple machines by checking out **www.mos.org/sln/Leonardo/ InventorsToolbox.html**.

Simple machines are commonly used. They are used in many tools from bicycles to can openers. In construction, simple machines help workers pull, raise, cut, attach, and increase or change the direction of force.

A lever is a common simple machine. It has a stiff bar and a fulcrum. The fulcrum is the point on the bar where the bar turns. An example of one type of lever is a see-saw. The fulcrum is in the center of this lever. When one end of the lever is pushed down, the other end goes up.

Levers are useful machines because they allow people to lift objects by placing them on one end of the bar and pushing down on the other end. To lift heavy objects, the fulcrum may be moved closer to the object. Less force is needed to lift objects that are closer to the fulcrum, making them easier to lift.

■ The claw on the back of a hammer is a type of lever. The top of the hammer acts as a fulcrum. Pulling on the long handle raises the shorter claw, making it easier to remove nails.

Throwing stones

The ancient Romans used simple machines to fight wars. They used catapults to throw huge rocks at their enemies. A catapult is a type of lever that uses a **pulley** system to load and launch the rocks.

How do cranes lift so much weight?

Cranes are easy to spot on a construction site. They are the machines with long mechanical arms that reach high into the air.

Cranes are used to **hoist** concrete, steel, large tools, and any other building materials that need to be moved from one place to another.

To secure a crane, a pad of thick concrete is poured. The base of the crane is anchored deep into this pad. The tower, or mast, of the crane is connected to the base. This mast supports the rest of the crane.

Once the crane is secured, it is ready to lift and move materials and tools. The operator sits in a cab and uses a combination of foot pedals and levers to lift heavy loads over short distances.

■ Cranes are used in many industries, including construction, shipping, and warehousing.

The motor and gear of the crane, called the slewing unit, are attached to the top of the mast. This allows the crane to swivel and turn. The slewing unit includes the jib, or arm, and a trolley. The jib is the part of the crane that supports the load. The trolley carries the load along the jib. A machinery arm is part of the slewing unit. The machinery arm contains the crane's electronic components and motors.

Heavy lifting

A crane can lift more weight if the load is carried closer to the center of the crane. A typical tower crane has a maximum span of 230 feet (70 m), a height of 262 feet (80 m), and a lifting capacity of 20 tons (18 t).

How are skyscrapers built?

Skyscrapers have come to define big city skylines. To many, it is amazing that such tall structures are sturdy enough to stay standing. In fact, taller skyscrapers are built every year.

find it quick

You can learn all about big structures, including skyscrapers, by checking out **www.pbs.org/wgbh/buildingbig**.

Skyscrapers grew out of the need to create the most business or living space on the smallest area of land. The challenge for early architects was to support all of the weight stacked upon the base of the building. As each new story was added, the pressure on every point below it became greater. This pressure is similar to stacking books on your head—your head, neck, and spine can only take so much weight. As buildings became taller, the walls of the lower floors, which had to support the weight of the floors above them became so thick that the rooms were no longer useable. It was only possible to construct buildings about 10 stories high using this method.

Taller structures became possible with the development of mass-produced steel and iron. Construction companies could now use long, solid **beams** of iron that were fairly light and easier to build with than concrete alone. Stronger—and even lighter—steel soon replaced iron. This opened the door to building taller skyscrapers. Today, skyscrapers are supported by steel beams, not thick walls.

■ Builders use a type of steel bar, called rebar, to make structures stronger.

Chicago was the site of the world's first skyscraper. In 1885, an architect named Major William Le Baron Jenney designed the Home Insurance Building. Made of steel and brick, it stood nine stories tall and had one basement. In 1891, two more stories were added to the structure.

Jenney's design changed the future of building. The load-carrying structural frame he created led to the development of the "Chicago skeleton" construction style. This style used a steel frame to support the weight of the building.

Look up

The tallest building in the United States is the Sears Tower in Chicago. It is 1,451 feet (442 m) tall.

How do skyscrapers withstand forces?

Skyscrapers are hundreds, or even thousands, of feet tall. Wind can be very powerful at these heights. Builders must plan for high winds when building these structures.

Skyscrapers are built on steel skeletons made from vertical columns and horizontal beams for support. This skeleton is called the superstructure. Where the columns meet the base, the pressure is distributed evenly underneath the building. This is the building's substructure. The substructure often consists of layers of horizontal beams anchored in a thick concrete base. The substructure is often wider than the building itself, so it can fully support the weight of the building. With this system, the walls of each floor only have to support that floor's weight.

How to best support a structure's weight is only one of many issues of concern for engineers. There are also outside forces, such as earthquakes and wind. For example, if a gusty wind blows, a skyscraper can sway from side to side like a tree. While this movement may not damage the structure, it can make the occupants of the building uneasy.

There is a way to lessen the effects of such forces. When a skyscraper is being constructed, crews tighten the points at which the vertical columns meet the horizontal beams in the frame. The building will then move as one solid object. As skyscrapers become even taller, this approach will not fix the problem. To keep taller buildings from swaying, engineers strengthen the building's core with steel supports and diagonal beams.

■ The vertical columns of the superstructure hold the weight of the entire building. The weight is transferred to the substructure.

Here is your challenge!

Build a model skyscraper by collecting cardboard boxes of different sizes. Place the widest box on the ground. This will be the base of your skyscraper. Stack the smaller boxes on top of the base. Use tape to hold the boxes together.

Push lightly on the top of your skyscraper. Does it fall over? Try arranging the boxes in a different order. Is one design stronger?

What do elevators do?

In some form or another, elevators have been in use since as early as 300 BC. The very first elevators only traveled between a few floors.

find it
quick

Visit **http://science.howstuff works.com/elevator.htm** to find out more about how elevators work.

The first power elevator in the United States was a hoist that raised and dropped between two floors in a New York City building. Safety devices were installed to prevent the car from dropping if the hoist rope broke. This design change made it possible for elevators to carry people. The first passenger elevator was soon operating in a New York City store.

Today, modern elevators carry thousands of pounds of freight and passengers up hundreds of floors, thousands of times each day. Without elevators, tall buildings would be useless. Even the most athletic visitor would shudder at the thought of walking up to the 99th floor.

As buildings have become taller, elevators have become faster. The Taipei 101 tower in Taiwan has elevators that race at a speed of 3,314 feet (1,010 m) per minute. That is more than three times faster than an airliner climbs after takeoff.

■ Elevators can be used to carry workers and materials at construction sites.

Going up

The first elevator used for transporting passengers was developed by Elisha Otis in 1857. Today, Otis is the world's largest builder of elevators, escalators, and moving walkways.

How are bridges built?

Anyone can build a basic bridge. If you have ever placed a plank of wood across a stream so you could cross without getting wet, you have built a bridge. However, bridges that support thousands of cars or people are much more complicated to build.

As bridges span greater distances, the forces acting on them increase. **Compression** and **tension** are two forces that bridge engineers face. On a bridge, excess compression can cause the surface to buckle, and excess tension can cause it to snap.

To avoid these problems, bridge designers spread the pressure out over a large area. For example, a beam bridge consists of a long, solid beam that is supported by columns on each end. Pressure, such as traffic traveling across the bridge, is supported by the columns. On this type of bridge, compression acts on the top side of the beam, causing it to shorten in width. This compression creates tension on the lower part of the beam, causing it to lengthen. To correct the forces of compression and tension, bridge designers increase the width of the beam.

Most often, steel or concrete beams are added to bridge designs in order to support the weight of the structure. Designers often add a lattice to the

■ There are more than 500,000 bridges in the United States. They span rivers, lakes, valleys, and even parts of oceans.

beams. A lattice is a system of triangles placed together to make the bridge more rigid. It further absorbs the forces of compression and tension.

Designs vary depending on the type of bridge, but the science of compression and tension is always in designers' minds.

Walking on eggs

In the early 17th century, a bridge was built in Lima, Peru. Instead of using water to mix the cement, the builders used 10,000 egg whites. The bridge, known as the Bridge of Eggs, is still standing.

How are dams built?

A dam is a structure that blocks water from flowing out of a particular area. Dams are use to prevent flooding, provide water for farmland, and generate electricity.

find it quick

Try building your own dam. Check out **http://pbskids.org/zoom/activities/ sci/buildadam.html** to find out how.

The first step in building a dam is to remove water from the construction site. **Cofferdams** are erected around an area of water, and the water is pumped out to keep the construction site dry. Concrete tunnels divert the water around the construction site. Construction workers can then build the framing for the foundation and pour concrete.

The pressure of water against the dam can destroy a poorly constructed or designed dam. The water exerts **hydrostatic pressure** that must be taken into consideration. Designers also consider uplift, the upward force caused by water pressure on the dam's foundation. Once these and other factors are incorporated into a design, a dam can be built.

Dams serve an important function, but there are serious drawbacks to them. Damming waterways can cause environmental problems. For example, animals may lose their water supply. Dams are also very expensive to build.

■ Dams can be controlled to release water at certain times. This raises or lowers the water level when necessary.

■ Once a dam is completed, the cofferdams can be removed. Sometimes, cofferdams are kept so they can be used for maintenance and repairs.

Air supply

Inflatable dams are a new way of controlling water. These dams have a thick rubber tube, a concrete foundation, and computerized controls. These dams can be inflated to about 9 feet (2.7 m) high. The dam can be deflated to allow flood waters to pass or to drain a body of water. Inflatable dams are useful because they deflate quickly and easily, preventing upstream flooding.

Who is Frank Gehry?

One of the best-known architects is Frank Gehry. He has created some of the most recognizable modern buildings in the world.

find it quick

Learn about Frank Gehry's life and work at **ww.sonyclassics.com/ sketchesoffrankgehry**.

Gehry studied architecture at the universities of Southern California and Harvard. He started his own architecture company in 1963.

Throughout his career, Gehry has employed many styles of architecture in his designs. His most notable structures break away from traditional styles and depend more on art and experimentation. Gehry performs many of his experiments on his own home before using them on other buildings. Many of his works can be recognized by their curved walls and roofs.

Gehry has built many private and public buildings and won many prestigious awards. In 1989, he was awarded the Pritzker Architecture Prize. This is one of the greatest achievements in architecture. Gehry's Guggenheim Museum in Bilbao, Spain, is considered a masterpiece of architecture.

■ Gehry designed the Dancing House in Prague, Czech Republic. The project was completed in 1996.

Frank Gehry was born in 1929, in Toronto, Canada. While growing up, he experimented with building structures out of household materials. This is how Gehry found his passion for architecture.

Rock on

In 2000, the Experience Music Project, a museum dedicated to rock music, opened in Seattle, Washington. Gehry designed the building to resemble a smashed electric guitar.

How do buildings keep people safe?

Researchers are developing ways to reduce the damage done to buildings by earthquakes. A material called magnetorheological fluid, or MR fluid, is being used to keep buildings steadier during earthquakes.

MR fluid can turn into a solid in the presence of a magnetic force. Once the force is removed, the substance becomes liquid again.

MR fluid is placed in containers called dampers. Dampers sit on the floor of a building. They are attached to braces and beams.

During minor earthquakes, the MR fluid inside the damper stiffens. This allows the building to sway with the vibrations, minimizing the shock. In the case of severe earthquakes, the MR fluid inside the dampers becomes solid. This prevents major damage to the structure of the building. MR fluid helps the dampers apply more force to stabilize the building. This technology saves lives and keeps buildings standing during earthquakes.

■ Dampers can be used to protect buildings, bridges, roads, oil rigs, and homes.

The big shake

There have been several major earthquakes in North America throughout history. In 1700, one of the most powerful earthquakes in history occurred over 600 miles (1,000 km) along the west coast of North America, killing entire villages of American Indians. The earthquake caused severe damage as far away as Japan.

Construction Careers

Structural Engineer

Structural engineers are often on site throughout the building process. It is their job to identify the best way to build a structure so that it will support its own weight and withstand outside forces. These engineers have a role in building a variety of structures, from homes to stadiums and oil rigs.

Structural engineers use math and physics to understand how parts of a building will affect each other. They must be familiar with different building materials. This way, they can choose the appropriate materials for the job. The construction process must follow the structural engineer's instructions at every step.

Architect

Architects design structures. They determine what is built on a construction site. Architects take years of university education to learn all they need to know about designing safe, useful, and appealing structures.

To begin, architects work with clients to develop ideas about what kind of structure to create. They take these ideas and create plans and models to show clients what the design will look like once it is finished. After the plans are approved, architects work closely with engineers and construction contractors to make sure all of the requirements are met and the local building codes are obeyed.

find it quick

Visit **www.constructmyfuture.com** to learn about many other careers available in the construction industry.

Young scientists at work
Build a Bridge

 Use the principles of bridge design discussed on pages 36 and 37 to build a small, sturdy bridge.

Materials:
Box of toothpicks, bag of mini-marshmallows, popsicle sticks, glue

What to do:
Poke a toothpick halfway through the sides of two marshmallows. Then, poke another toothpick halfway through the top of each marshmallow. Poke the other ends of the toothpicks into another marshmallow. This forms a triangle with a marshmallow at each point. Continue connecting toothpicks and marshmallows until you have three triangles. These will make up one side of the bridge. Repeat this process to build the other side of the bridge.

Place one side flat on the table. Then, place toothpicks through each corner of the triangles. Connect the other side of the bridge to these toothpicks. This completes the frame of the bridge.

To build the roadway, glue popsicle sticks to the bottom section of the bridge. Test the strength of the bridge with items from around your house.

Take a construction test

1. What is magnetorheological (MR) fluid used for?

2. Why do builders use blueprints?

3. Name three buildings designed by Frank Gehry. What makes these buildings special?

4. What are the two forces that affect the safety and design of a bridge?

5. What is the advantage of pressure-treated lumber?

ANSWERS: 1. Magnetorheological (MR) fluid is used to stabilize buildings during earthquakes. **2.** Builders use blueprints to read the layout and measurements of a construction site. Blueprints tell the builder where to put walls, doors, windows, plumbing, and many other items important to the structure. **3.** Three buildings created by Frank Gehry are the Guggenheim Museum in Bilbao, Spain, the Experience Music Project in Seattle, Washington, and the Dancing House in Prague, Czech Republic. These buildings are unique because of their curved walls and roofs. **4.** Compression and tension are two forces that affect the safety and design of a bridge. **5.** Pressure-treated lumber can last much longer than untreated wood. It is more durable in wind, rain, snow, heat, and other conditions that cause wood decay.

Fast Facts

The largest structure ever built is the Great Wall of China. It stretches about 4,000 miles (6,400 km) along China's northern border.

The Pentagon, in Langley, Virginia, is the largest office building in the world. It contains 34 acres (13.8 hectares) of space.

The Channel Tunnel links Great Britain to mainland Europe. It covers 31 miles (50 km), 23 miles (37 km) of which are underwater.

The Statue of Liberty took nine years to build in France. It was taken apart and shipped to New York, where it was reassembled.

Grand Coulee Dam in Washington is the largest concrete structure in the United States.

Scientists in Japan discovered a home that was built 500,000 years ago. It was built by an ancient ancestor of humans.

The sides of the pyramids of Giza face directly north, south, east, and west. Historians believe the Egyptians may have used the stars or the Sun to find the directions.

In some areas of northern China, people have built entire towns in caves. The cave homes are called "yaodong."

Antoni Gaudi began building the Sagrada Familia church in Barcelona, Spain, in 1882. It will take builders until 2041 to complete the project.

The Burj Dubai skyscraper in Dubai, United Arab Emirates, will be more than 2,625 feet (800 m) tall. This makes it the world's tallest structure.

Glossary

beams: large, long horizontal support pieces of a building

cofferdams: temporary, watertight structures that keep dam building sites dry

compression: act of putting pressure on something

contractors: people who do a certain job for an agreed price on a construction site

detonated: set off, as in an explosion

hoist: lift with ropes or pulleys

hydrostatic pressure: the force water exerts while at rest

imploding: bursting inward

incompressible: unable to be squeezed into a smaller space

innovations: new ways of doing things

pistons: moving parts that slide up and down within a cylinder filled with liquid

plantation: land on which crops, such as sugar or cotton, are grown

pulley: a simple machine using a rope running along a grooved wheel to lift an object

synthetic: man-made through a chemical process

tension: act of pulling or stretching something

Index